Healthy Snacks

BY BETH BENCE REINKE, MS, RD

The Child's World

Published by The Child's World®
1980 Lookout Drive • Mankato, MN 56003-1705
800-599-READ • www.childsworld.com

Acknowledgments
The Child's World®: Mary Berendes, Publishing Director
Red Line Editorial: Editorial direction
The Design Lab: Design
Amnet: Production
Photographs ©: Front cover: BrandX; Sergii Figurnyi/Shutterstock
Images; FoodIcons; FoodIcons, 3, 6, 7, 8, 9, 11, 12, 14, 15, 17,
23; BrandX Images, 3, 10, 13, 16, 20; GeneralFoodImages, 4;
choosemyplate.gov, 5; Beth Bence Reinke, 21

ISBN: 978-1623236007
LCCN: 2013931336

Printed in the United States of America
Mankato, MN
July, 2013
PA02178

ABOUT THE AUTHOR

Beth Bence Reinke is a registered dietitian with a master's degree in nutrition from Penn State University. She uses her background in education and pediatric nutrition to help kids learn about healthy eating. Beth is a member of the Academy of Nutrition and Dietetics, a children's author, a magazine writer, and a columnist for her favorite sport, NASCAR.

Table of Contents

CHAPTER ONE

Fun Fruits and Vegetables

It's snack time! Coach passes out cups of water and then opens a snack cooler. Mia takes a yogurt. Jake grabs peanut butter crackers. Tina cannot decide between apple slices and carrot sticks, so she takes both. Healthy snacks like these take away hunger between meals.

Snacks give kids energy and help them grow. Healthy snacks come from the five food groups: fruits, vegetables, grains, **protein**, and dairy. The MyPlate guide has a plate and cup that shows how much to eat from each food group. MyPlate helps kids make smart choices for meals and snacks.

▲ **Vegetables are healthy anytime snacks.**

▶ **Opposite page: Use the MyPlate diagram to make healthy eating choices.**

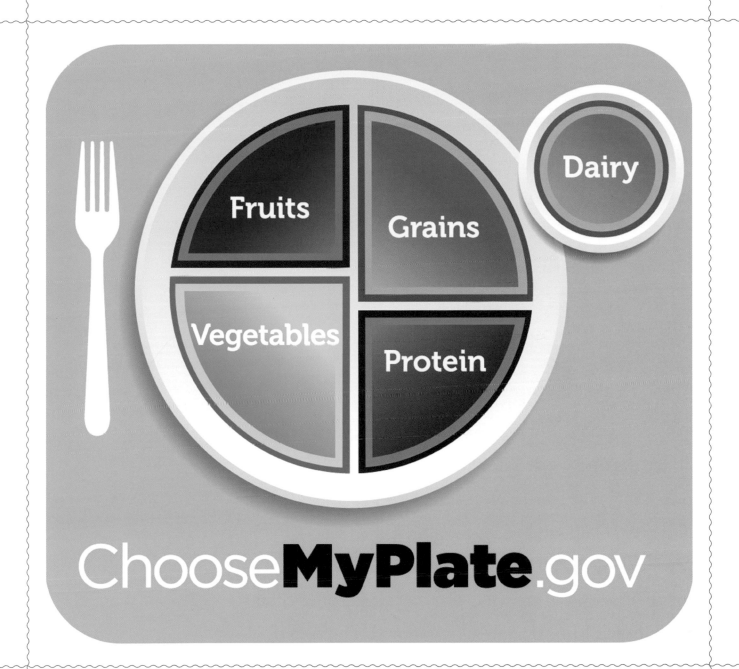

ChooseMyPlate.gov

◄ Fruits are full of fiber, vitamins, and minerals.

Fruits and vegetables are colorful snacks. Some are crunchy or leafy. Others are sweet or juicy. Together, fruits and vegetables fill half of the MyPlate plate. Fruits and vegetables contain **fiber**, **vitamins**, and **minerals**. These are substances you need for healthy **digestion**, a strong body, and a

FRUIT OR FAKE?

Have you ever seen a cereal box with the word *fruity* on it? How about fruit punch or fruit-flavored candies? Fruit-flavored drinks and brightly colored candies look pretty. Colorful cereal might even smell fruity. But these foods contain only a small amount of fruit. Some have no fruit at all! Many fruity snacks and drinks are full of sugar. They have fake colors and flavors instead of real fruit. Forget fake fruity foods. Grab real fruit instead!

▶ Your grocery store has lots of healthy options.

sharp mind. Choose fruits and vegetables with bright colors like red strawberries and yellow squash. Try green broccoli and orange sweet potatoes. Want to taste a rainbow of flavors this week? Snack on colorful fruits and vegetables!

You can find all sorts of fruits and vegetables at the grocery store. Fresh fruits are whole, like bananas and apples. Some come in cans, like sliced peaches or pineapple chunks. Others are frozen, like blueberries and strawberries. Some fruits are dried, such as raisins and dried cranberries. Vegetables also come fresh, canned, or frozen. Look for fresh vegetables like broccoli and carrots in the produce section of your grocery store. Other vegetables may be canned, like green beans and

corn. Common frozen vegetables include spinach and green peas.

Fruits and vegetables are tasty snacks alone or with other foods. Toss dried fruit with nuts for a snack mix. Blend fruit with yogurt for a smoothie. Put raw veggies on a plate. Add a little cup of dip. You made a crisp and creamy snack!

Together, fruits and vegetables are part of a healthy diet. Kids four to eight years old need to eat 1 1/2 cups of fruit and 1 to 1 1/2 cups of vegetables every day. One cup of 100 percent fruit juice or 1/2 cup of dried fruit counts as 1 cup of fruit. A cup of raw or cooked vegetables, 1 cup of vegetable juice, and 2 cups of leafy greens like lettuce all count as 1 cup of vegetables.

◄ **Fruit smoothies are sweet and healthy treats.**

▶ **Whole grains are full of vitamins and minerals.**

CHAPTER TWO

Good-for-You Grains

Grains come from seeds of plants such as wheat, oats, barley, and rice. Substances in grains called **carbohydrates** give your body energy. Grains fill one quarter of the MyPlate plate. There are two kinds of grains: **whole grains** and **refined grains**.

Foods made with whole grains are good for you. They contain fiber from the whole grain seed. Whole grains are loaded with vitamins and minerals. The MyPlate guide says half the grains you eat should be whole grains. Some whole-grain snacks are crunchy to munch. Try popcorn or whole-grain crackers. For a softer snack, spread peanut butter on a whole-wheat tortilla and roll it up.

WHOLE GRAINS

A grain seed has three parts. Two parts contain the grain's fiber, vitamins, and minerals. Another part contains starch, a carbohydrate. While whole grains contain all three parts of the seed, refined grains contain only the part with starch. That is why whole-grain foods are healthier. Look at the ingredients list to tell if a food has whole grains. If the word *whole* is before the first ingredient, it is a whole-grain food.

◄ Popcorn is a healthy, whole-grain snack.

▲ Cupcakes are junk food and should not be eaten frequently.

Unlike whole grains, refined grains have had their fiber, vitamins, and minerals removed. White pasta and white bread are examples of refined grains. Doughnuts, cookies, and cakes are usually made with refined grains, too. Foods like these are called **junk foods**. They contain lots of **fats** and added sugars. Junk foods are treats for special days like holidays or birthdays. MyPlate does not have a space for treats. They are not foods to eat every day.

Kids ages four to eight need to eat 4 or 5 ounces of grains each day. A slice of bread, 1 cup of ready-to-eat cereal, and 1/2 cup of rice, pasta, or cooked cereal all count as 1 ounce of grains.

CHAPTER THREE

Powerful Proteins

The body needs protein to stay healthy. Proteins contain the building blocks for strong muscles and bones. Proteins also help keep blood and skin healthy. You should fill about one quarter of your plate with protein foods. You can find protein in meats like beef, pork, chicken, turkey, and fish.

◄ Turkey and eggs are good sources of protein.

► Opposite page: Milk is a great way to add protein to your diet.

Eggs, dried beans, nuts, seeds, and foods in the dairy group also contain protein.

Most protein foods also contain fats. Fats are not shown on MyPlate, but our bodies need them for good health. **Oils** are healthy fats. Oils are found in protein foods like seafood, seeds, and nuts. **Solid fats** found in meats and dairy foods are less healthy than oils. Choose chicken and turkey more often because they have less solid fats. MyPlate reminds us to eat more healthy oils and less solid fat. You can eat protein snacks with healthy oils more often. Try walnuts, sunflower seeds, peanut butter, and tuna fish.

Many yummy snacks are in the protein group. Try spreading peanut

▲ **Want a snack with a protein punch? Choose mixed nuts.**

MOVE YOUR MUSCLES!
Kids need 60 minutes of active play every day. That's because your body is made to bend, stretch, hop, and scoot. Eating healthy snacks gives you energy to run fast and jump high. Protein snacks help build muscles to help you move.

What is your favorite activity? Playing soccer? Dancing? Dribbling a basketball? There are lots of fun ways to be active. All kinds of movements keep your muscles strong. Be sure to move your muscles every day.

butter on whole-grain crackers for a crunchy snack. A hard-boiled egg or a scoop of tuna salad is a filling after-school treat. Need to take a snack along? Mix nuts and seeds together. Stash them in your backpack.

Kids ages four to eight need 3 or 4 ounces of protein foods each day. One egg, 1 ounce of meat or fish, a 1/4 cup of cooked beans, 1 tablespoon of peanut butter, and 1/2 ounce of nuts or seeds all count as 1 ounce of protein.

CHAPTER FOUR

Delicious Dairy

Dairy foods are foods that come from milk. Milk contains protein. It also has vitamins and minerals that help build strong bones and teeth. The MyPlate guide includes one serving of dairy with every meal. Dairy foods make cool and creamy snacks. Open the fridge and grab a low-fat yogurt cup or some string cheese. Yum!

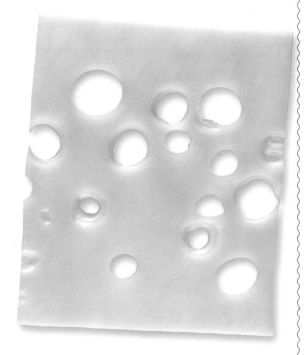

◄ **Cheese is a delicious dairy snack.**

▶ **Opposite page: Yogurt is a sweet snack with fruit and protein.**

Did you know there is more than one kind of cow's milk? The grocery store has four kinds with different amounts of fat. Whole milk has the most fat. Young children need whole milk. The extra fat in whole milk helps babies and toddlers grow properly. Older kids can switch to milk with less fat.

There are three choices with less fat: 2 percent milk, 1 percent milk, and skim milk. Skim milk is also called non-fat milk because it has almost no fat. The fat in milk is solid fat, just like butter. The MyPlate guide recommends we eat or drink less solid fat.

If you drink whole milk, you gulp down 2 teaspoons of butter in each cup. But 2 percent milk has

▼ **Milk is a creamy and nutritious snack.**

DRINK UP!

Need a drink to wash down your healthy snack? Milk is a nutritious drink. Water is a healthy choice, too. Every sip helps give your body the fluid it needs. A small box of 100 percent juice is an okay drink. But soda and other sugary drinks are not healthy drinks. They have too much sugar. Reach for milk, water, or 100 percent fruit juice when you need a drink to slurp with your snacks.

only 1 teaspoon of butter per cup. A cup of 1 percent milk has 1/2 teaspoon, and skim milk has only a tiny bit. Want to drink less butter? Switch to lower fat milk!

Kids ages four to eight need 2 cups of milk or other dairy foods each day. A cup of yogurt, 2 ounces of processed cheese like American cheese, and 1 1/2 ounces of natural cheese, like cheddar or Swiss, all count the same as 1 cup of milk.

Hands-on Activity: Rainbow Dippers

These rainbow-colored pepper shapes are fun to eat with veggie dip.

What You'll Need:

A knife, small cookie cutters, and four large bell peppers (one each of red, orange, yellow, and green)

Directions:

1. First, wash the peppers and pat them dry with paper towels. Then, ask an adult to cut the peppers in half from top to bottom. Remove the seeds and stem.

2. Next, push cookie cutters into the inside of the peppers to cut out shapes. Press firmly to break through the peppers' thin skins. Arrange pepper shapes on a plate and serve with dip.

Glossary

carbohydrates (kar-bo-HY-drayts): Carbohydrates are parts of food that provide energy to the body. Fiber, starches, and sugars are all carbohydrates.

digestion (dye-JES-chun): Digestion is when the body breaks down food so it can use it. Fiber in fruits and vegetables helps with digestion.

fats (fats): Fats are parts of food that provide energy to the body. Fats help the body use some of the vitamins found in food.

fiber (FYE-ber): Fiber is the part of plant foods the body cannot break down. Fiber helps with healthy digestion.

junk foods (JUNK foodz): Junk foods are foods that are not healthy. Foods that are high in fat or sugar, like cakes and doughnuts, are junk foods.

minerals (MIN-er-ulz): Minerals are substances found in foods. Minerals help the body stay healthy.

oils (OY-ulz): Oils are fats that are liquid at room temperature. Oils in our foods can come from plants and seafood.

protein (PRO-teen): Protein is a part of food that provides energy and contains building blocks used by the whole body. Proteins are found in meat, nuts, and seeds.

refined grains (ree-FYEND graynz): Refined grains are foods made with only the part of the grain seed that contains starch. White bread and white pasta are refined grains.

solid fats (SOL-id fats): Solid fats are fats that are solid at room temperature. Solid fats are found in meats and dairy foods.

vitamins (VYE-tuh-minz): Vitamins are substances found in foods that help the body stay healthy. Vitamins are found in fruits and vegetables.

whole grains (hol GRAYNZ): Whole grains are foods made with all three parts of the grain seed. Fiber, minerals, and vitamins are found in whole grains.

To Learn More

BOOKS

Mayo Clinic. *The Mayo Clinic Kids' Cookbook: 50 Favorite Recipes for Fun and Healthy Eating*. Intercourse, PA: Good Books, 2012.

Wilensky, Amy. *Healthy Snacks for Kids: Recipes for Nutritious Bites at Home or on the Go*. Guilford, CT: Knack, 2010.

WEB SITES

Visit our Web site for links about healthy snacks: **childsworld.com/links**

Note to Parents, Teachers, and Librarians: We routinely verify our Web links to make sure they are safe and active sites. So encourage your readers to check them out!

Index